The beauty of New Zealand derives often from a happy blend of opposites, the native and the introduced, the wild and the peaceful. In the Mangawharariki Valley in the North Island's Rangitikei district, open, peaceful pasture contrasts pleasingly with the brooding green bush, undisturbed by human beings. But there are reminders, even on the pastureland, that many New Zealand landscapes have changed since human beings first occupied these islands a thousand years ago. The "cabbage tree", which looks like a palm but is actually a member of the lily family, still adorns the cleared land. Cabbage trees are beloved by many New Zealanders because they are so distinctive of New Zealand landscapes. And this is a landscape which in many ways could only be New Zealand.

THE BEAUTY
OF
NEW ZEALAND

Photographs by Warren Jacobs
Text by John Wilson

KOWHAI
PUBLISHING LTD

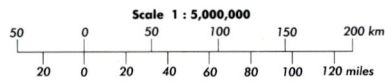

INTRODUCTION

The commonplace saying that "beauty is in the eye of the beholder" has special relevance in New Zealand. What appears beautiful to one person in a scene or view may seem ordinary or even unpleasant to another. To satisfy everyone's tastes, a country needs to be extraordinary. New Zealand is an extraordinary country. Its complex geological history (it sits astride one of the most active points on the earth's surface where the Pacific and Australian tectonic plates are in contact), its shape (long and thin; 1,600 kilometres long but only 450 wide at its widest point, and mostly much narrower than that), and its mid-oceanic setting (which mean rapidly changing weather but a generally mild climate) have all combined to produce a succession of landscapes of such variety that everyone will find beauty in some part of New Zealand if not another. New Zealand is unusual, too, in being mostly a raw, new land. The first human beings landed on its shores a mere thousand years ago; to reach Aotearoa/New Zealand both Maori and Pakeha settlers made prodigiously long voyages and the country remains only lightly settled by international standards (with about three and a half million people on islands roughly the same in area as the islands of Britain or Japan). Vast areas of New Zealand have been altered, sometimes to advantage, sometimes for the worse, by human activities; but large areas, too, remain in a relatively untouched, pristine state. It is the ready access in New Zealand to natural landscapes and environments as well as the variety of the landforms and scenery that make New Zealand an extraordinary place.

Title spread, preceding: To some the mountain landscapes of the South Island are austere, even bleak, frightening in their scale and immensity. But the serene waters of Lake Alexandrina (small neighbour of the Mackenzie Country's Lake Tekapo), and its fringe of willows, "yellowing autumn's joy", soften and humanise the vast open spaces of the high country.

SOUTH ISLAND

The beauty of the South Island is the beauty of open spaces, of nature little changed by human activity, of a world largely spared the disfiguring excesses of modern industrial civilisation. Somewhat larger than the North Island, the South Island has far fewer people—a few more than 880,000 compared to the North Island's 2.5 million. Although there are settled, farming landscapes in the South Island, a handful of cities and scattered towns, it is the grandeur of almost empty mountain spaces, the beauty of wild places and of sometimes wild weather, that remain in the memories of people who have travelled through the South Island. Compared to the North Island, the South is a place of grand scale and almost of excesses. It has the country's highest mountains and largest glaciers (in the Southern Alps), but also its largest area of flat land (the Canterbury Plains). Nowhere in New Zealand are the contrasts in the landscape more abrupt and apparent than in the transition from the wet, forested West Coast to the dry, semi-arid mountains and plains of the eastern "rain shadow" areas, in the lea of the Southern Alps. Though good roads traverse much of the South Island, there are still satisfyingly large tracts of country with no more than simple mountain huts and rough walking trails as reminders that this is not the completely virgin, untouched land it can so often seem, often from the very edge of a highway.

The contrasts that the South Island affords in its landscapes are apparent in views from opposite ends of the island. At Aparima in Southland *(this page, inset above)* some of the country's flock of more than fifty million sheep graze lush pastures against a background of wild mountains which still hold winter's snow in their high basins. The scale of the country is such that the stately march of pylons carrying electric power from the Manapouri power station to the aluminium smelter at Bluff do not seem intrusive or disfiguring. More welcoming and intimate, the beauty at Anchorage, in Nelson's Abel Tasman National Park *(left, opposite page)* is found in the appealing curve of the beach and the blending of colours where bush-clad hills finger down to sandy beaches that front blue seas. The park was named after the Dutch navigator who was the first recorded European visitor to New Zealand waters.

The introduction of many travellers to the South Island is the port town of Picton *(opposite page, top),* at the innermost reach of Queen Charlotte Sound, a good distance in from the open sea. After crossing a sometimes tempestuous Cook Strait, ferry boats from Wellington thread their way through picturesque Tory Channel and Queen Charlotte Sound to berth at Picton. A war memorial on the waterfront is typical of most New Zealand towns, commemorating those who fought and died in far-off battlefields this century. No battles have been fought on New Zealand soil since the Land Wars of the 1860s and 1870s.

The Marlborough Sounds are drowned river valleys, a complex of waterways, islands, peninsulas and peaceful bays, like Crail Bay *(this page, above).* Though some roads thread their ways across the often steep hills of the Sounds, for many bays the easiest and sometimes the only access is by boat.

Across Tasman Bay, to the west of the Marlborough Sounds, the smallest of New Zealand's national parks, Abel Tasman, protects an appealing stretch of coastline, with sandy beaches and rocky foreshores separating blue sea and green bush, as at Te Pukatea Bay *(opposite page, lower right)* where a spreading tree fern gives the scene an almost tropical look.

Inland from the Abel Tasman National Park, the rich soils of the mild, sun-warmed Riwaka Valley *(opposite page, lower left)* support intensive horticulture and fruit-growing. This productive, closely settled land is literally within minutes by car from the bush-clad hills and secluded beaches of the Abel Tasman National Park.

At the western edge of the Abel Tasman National Park, at Ligar Bay *(above)* a tall obelisk on a headland commemorates the brief visit of the Dutch navigator Abel Tasman to these waters in 1642. He did not land and four of his men were killed in an encounter at sea with local Maori. New Zealand's windy, maritime climate makes for sometimes rough seas and cloudy skies, but also make the country one of spectacular sunsets.

The Abel Tasman National Park lies between more populous Tasman Bay and Nelson city and Golden Bay, an area of remote beauty with farms running up into wild hills. Up the Aorere River, the main river flowing into Golden Bay, swim whitebait, the young of several species of fish which are caught in fine-meshed nets *(opposite page, lower)* and end up as a delicacy on Golden Bay tables.

The strong, vigorous landforms of a young country, still being thrust up by geological forces, are evident in the creased hills of the upper Riwaka Valley *(left),* inland from Tasman and Golden Bays.

The coastal walk in the Abel Tasman National Park passes Torrent Bay *(left)*. This walk is popular, but those making it can still experience the beauty of nature without the distractions of "civilisation" and its crowds interfering with their appreciation of unspoiled country.

New Zealand's beauty is seen in broad sweeps of landscape; it is also seen in the intimate detail of wind-rippled sand on the dunes Wharariki beach *(this page, top)* which are found on many stretches of New Zealand's long shoreline.

The complexity of the Marlborough Sounds, where the South Island's north-eastern tip frays into the wild seas of Cook Strait, are evident looking down on Kenepuru and Pelorous Sounds from the air *(this page, above)*. Pelorous Sound retains fame from the early years of this century when a dolphin "Pelorous Jack" guided boats in and out of the sound.

Looking down on the Kaikoura Mountains in winter *(opposite)*, the extent of the South Island's magnificent mountain wilderness is apparent. Hugging the east coast of the South Island, the Kaikoura Ranges are the most northerly of the maze of peaks and ranges which to the south and west become the Southern Alps, the central chain of highest mountains.

The small town of Kaikoura *(above)* sits on a narrow coastal plain beneath the Kaikoura Mountains. Off Kaikoura, the sea floor plunges as profoundly deep as the mountains rise dramatically high. These nutrient-rich, deep waters are frequented by whales and other sea mammals, including dolphins and seals. The proximity of such deep waters to the shore makes Kaikoura one of the easiest places in the world to see these survivors of the now-banned sealing and whaling industries. Happily the threatened creatures are making a comeback and Kaikoura, founded as a whaling town, now prospers from nature tourism.

15

Strung down the centre of the South Island is a series of wonderful mountain lakes, most the legacy of the great glaciers of past ice ages, which scoured out deep valleys and retreated leaving natural dams of moraine. In Maori tradition the lakes were scooped out by a legendary hero, Rakaihautu, with his ko (digging stick). The most northerly of these Southern Lakes are Lake Rotoiti and Lake Rotoroa *(above)*. The bush-fringed beauty of both of these lakes is protected in the Nelson Lakes National Park.

The Southern Alps lie athwart prevailing westerly winds (the "roaring forties" of the days of sailing ships). These winds, hitting the barrier of mountains, drop enormous quantities of rain and snow on the west, then blow dry and hot to the east. The high precipitation on the West Coast supports some of the finest temperate rain forests in the world. On the Minehaha Track at Fox Glacier *(opposite)*, visitors are deep in primeval forest within minutes of stepping from their cars or buses.

The west coast of the South Island has an extremely high rainfall, and when sheets of rain lash in from the Tasman Sea it can be a dour, depressing place. But in favoured times of the year the Coast also enjoys long periods of settled, sunny weather, when the coastline north of Punakaiki *(above),* with its abundant vegetation presents a smiling face.

The Tasman Sea, subjected to strong westerly winds, is often rough. Huge swells coast in from the open sea to break on the rocky coast. Nature has worked to dramatic effect as sculptor at Punakaiki *(opposite)* where layered limestone, subject to the seas relentless pounding, has weathered to the strong forms of the prosaically but aptly named Pancake Rocks.

Westland has a narrow coastal strip of river flats and bush-covered hills lying between its wild, open coast and the precipitous, snow-covered Alps. Parts of this coastal strip are made up of complex old moraines and nestled in hollows among these moraines are quiet, calm lakes, like Mapourika *(above)*, many fringed with forest and famous for the reflections of the mountains in their still waters.

Parts of Westland's coastal strip are farmed, giving an attractive juxtaposition of lofty ranges with farm houses and outbuildings. Near Whataroa, a farm building *(opposite page, below)* close to the bush, typically built of corrugated iron and unpainted, is dominated by the peaks of the high alps.

The abrupt descent from high, vast snowfields to forested lowlands make the Fox *(left)* and Franz Josef Glaciers unique in New Zealand. Their terminal faces lie well below the level where the forest grows dense and green. These are the remnants of once mightier glaciers which, in earlier "ice ages", coalesced to form an ice shelf at the toes of the mountains.

21

South of the Glaciers, the Haast Pass highway skirts Lake Moeraki *(above)* in the almost untouched wilderness which runs from South Westland into Fiordland National Park, designated a world heritage area. The feathery toi toi which fringes the lake edge is a graceful New Zealand relation of pampas grass.

One of the most often visited of South Westland's bush-fringed lakes is Lake Matheson *(opposite page, below)*, justly famous for one of New Zealand's finest views, the highest peaks of the Southern Alps reflected in the lake's still waters. The view is as wonderful at dawn, when morning mist wreathes the lower slopes of the mountains, as in the evening, when the peaks reflect the setting sun.

Like the Fox Glacier, the Franz Josef *(opposite page, top right)* sends a long tongue of ice down a narrow valley. Sensitive to the weather, which affects the amount of snow which falls on the glacier's snowfields, the Franz Josef advances and retreats decade by decade. An advance in the 1990s sent ice churning through rocks and bulldozing bush growing on ground left bare by an earlier retreat. Guides lead intrepid visitors onto the ice of both the Fox and Franz Josef Glaciers.

The snowfields which funnel into the Fox and Franz Josef Glaciers are spectacularly vast, high and lonely places. Mountaineers who venture onto them rope themselves together for protection should anyone fall into one of the huge, sinister crevasses that cut across the snowfields *(opposite page, top left)* but tourists are landed safely on level areas of the snowfields in small planes with skis.

Some New Zealanders believe that the country's extensive exotic forests disfigure New Zealand's beauty, but some of the older exotic forests now have a beauty of their own. Noble conifers in the long-established plantations at Hanmer in North Canterbury *(above)* provide places to walk which compare favourably with untouched native bush.

The township of Hanmer *(opposite page, below)* grew up around hot springs on one edge of a broad inter-montane basin. Such wide, open areas of flat land, ringed by rugged mountains, are typical of the high country of the eastern South Island. The hills are covered in tussock grass because the climate is, generally, too dry to support forest. This spectacular view over Hanmer and its basin is gained by a short walk up Conical Hill, immediately above the town.

Inland from Hanmer are the forested valleys of the Spenser Mountains, where grassy flats are prettily enclosed by native beech forest. On such a flat in the Ada Valley *(opposite page, above)* a tramper walking the St James Walkway pauses to boil a billy.

No New Zealand city has the breath-taking beauty of Paris, the historic interest of London or the drama of New York, but in Christchurch old buildings and new blend to provide pleasing urban prospects under Canterbury's wide sky. Victoria Square *(above)*, with a statue of the Queen who gave the Square its name presiding in one corner, is ringed in the background by, from left to right, the city's Law Courts, the Parkroyal Hotel and the Town Hall.

Christchurch cultivates English traditions—it was founded as an Anglican settlement by men determined to re-create England in the Antipodes. The city now has its own Town Cryer *(left)* who announces events at the Arts Centre market and elsewhere round the city. The Arts Centre is a fine group of stone Gothic buildings which once housed Canterbury University. The buildings give substance to the city's claim to have an English air.

A small market also flourishes in Cathedral Square, at the heart of Christchurch, where the Gothic Revival Anglican Cathedral *(above)* is still a commanding presence, though its tower and spire are now over-topped by modern buildings. Built over several decades and finally completed in 1904, the Cathedral is the undisputed symbol of Christchurch.

Christchurch is proud of its gardens, both public and private. It has one of the world's premier Botanic Gardens and in summer many of its residential streets are horticultural showcases. At the Ilam Homestead, now incorporated into the new campus of the University of Canterbury, a once-private garden has a world-renowned collection of azaleas *(right)* which make a superb display in spring.

Though Christchurch is built mostly over a flat corner of the Canterbury Plains, immediately south of the city the Port Hills, the remnant rim of an old volcano, shelter Lyttelton Harbour, an eroded crater invaded by the sea. Though ships regularly sail in and out to the port of Lyttelton, and many people now live in the harbour basin, Lyttelton Harbour is still scenically attractive. The length of the harbour is seen to advantage from Governors Bay *(right)*, a short drive over Dyers Pass from the city of Christchurch.

The road which runs west from Christchurch over the Southern Alps via Arthurs Pass is one of the most scenic drives in the country. It traverses the flat plains of Canterbury, the basins of the drier eastern ranges, the rugged mountains of the Alps, and then the forested valleys of Westland. An hour from Christchurch, the road passes through the Castle Hill Basin, where Highland cattle graze *(above)*. Snow on the Torlesse Range is evidence that the cattle need to be of such hardy stock.

On the drive from Christchurch to the Mackenzie Country and Mount Cook, the hill country between Geraldine and Fairlie *(opposite page)* comes as a relief after the flat plains. Sheep graze contentedly on pastures sheltered by plantations and shelter belts of exotic trees from the nor'-west winds which sweep hot and dry from the mountains beyond.

After passing through this hill country, the road descends into the Fairlie Basin *(left)* with its pleasing prospects of rolling pasture and mountains. The Fairlie Basin is another of the inter-montane basins, ringed by high ranges, that are typical of the mountainous South Island.

Some crops are grown in South Canterbury, but like most other South Island farmers, those of South Canterbury rely for a good part of their income on sheep *(above)*, whose meat is exported, frozen, to many other countries and whose wool is another mainstay of New Zealand's export economy.

The first of the Great Southern Lakes which travellers down the centre of the South Island encounter, soon after crossing Burkes Pass into the Mackenzie Country, is also one of the most attractive. The blue waters of Lake Tekapo *(left)* have the Southern Alps as their distant backdrop. The wide skies of the Mackenzie Country give rise to dramatic cloud formations and sunsets over the lake *(right)*. On the shore of the lake stands one of New Zealand's best-known buildings, the Church of the Good Shepherd *(above)*. Its rugged beauty (it is built of boulders collected from the lake shore) suits its remarkable setting perfectly. The lake occupies a vast hollow in undulating downs and terraces of golden tussock. Though a hydro-electric control structure now contain the lake, it owes its origin to the natural dam of an old moraine.

Nature's most vigorous sculptor on the South Island has been glacier ice. Much vaster than today's remnants, ancient glaciers carved blocks of rock into cirques, ridges and jagged peaks, then bulldozed the scoured debris into bold forms. Across the Mackenzie Country are wonderful landforms *(above)* left by the glaciers, their bold shapes now softened by a carpet of tussock grassland. The yellows and golds of these grasslands, varying in different light, are one of the glories of the South Island's high country.

Where the golden tussock reaches down to the blue waters of Lake Alexandrina, *(right)* there is a beauty few other parts of New Zealand can rival, especially with the fringe of autumn willows around the lake shore. A lucky few have holiday homes by the lake and spend idyllic summer weeks swimming, fishing or boating. But to preserve the lake's tranquillity, power boats are banned.

The beauty of the highest mountains of the Southern Alps is austere but dramatic. Rocky ridges culminate in the mile-long summit ridge of Aoraki/Mount Cook *(above)*. The whole ridge is higher than any other summit and the High Peak reaches 3754 metres into the sky. To the right is a section of New Zealand's largest glacier, the Tasman, which flows for twenty-nine kilometres from high snowfields north of Aoraki/Mount Cook itself to a moraine-covered terminal face that is not far from the settlement of Mount Cook and its premier hotel, the Hermitage.

Some of the finest views of Aoraki/Mount Cook are gained a little "down country", from the shores of Lake Pukaki *(opposite page, top)*. When late evening light bathes the flanks of three of New Zealand's highest mountains, La Perouse, Aoraki/Mount Cook and Tasman, the sight is incomparable.

A little further down the shores of the lake, near the Ferintosh sheep station *(opposite page, bottom)*, nature has used a vivid palette to superb effect. The brilliant turquoise of the lake (its colour resulting from the finely ground "rock flour" suspended in the water), the green of grasslands and trees and the various coloured wild flowers all contrast with the pure white of cloud and distant snowfield. The clouds warn of an approaching westerly and the scene may soon be blotted out by grey cloud and torrential rain sweeping over the faces of the mountains.

Each of the Southern Lakes has its own character. Lake Wakatipu *(left, opposite page)* has ice-shaped mountains rising more steeply from its shores than the lakes of the open Mackenzie Country to the north. Here the blue waters of Meiklejohn Bay, on Lake Wakatipu, just nudge into a view dominated by Mount Earnslaw beyond the head of the lake.

Many visitors head for Queenstown, on the shores of Lake Wakatipu, to ski, to ride wild rivers in jetboats or rubber rafts, or even to jump from high bridges with rubber cords attached to their feet! But others come just to contemplate the area's scenery and the quiet beauty which can be found on country roads *(above)* not far from busy Queenstown itself.

The Remarkable Mountains form the spectacular eastern skyline of Queenstown. But the Remarkables provide visitors to Queenstown with more than just a superb backdrop to the town. Skiers flock to broad basins below the rocky crest of the Remarkables that catch winter's snow *(left)*, to enjoy their sport. The Remarkables ski-field is companion to nearby Coronet Peak. Together the fields help give Queenstown pre-eminence in a sport that is popular among New Zealanders as well as with overseas visitors.

New Zealand's mountains can be forbidding and stern and show little mercy on those who take their dangers lightly. Only skilled and well-equipped mountaineers would venture into the Darran Mountains of northern Fiordland *(above, right)* when they wear their mantle of winter snow. But this view of them can be seen in safety and comfort on a scenic flight between Queenstown and Milford Sound.

In summer, the mountains seem gentler and more hospitable and their beauty less harsh. New Zealand's native flowers are not, by and large, ostentatious or flamboyant, but here where they stud a fell-field close to Lake Castalia *(above, left)* in the upper Wilkin Valley of the Mount Aspiring National Park, their lack of showy form or bright colour seems not to matter. Most of the peaks visible at the heads of Lakes Wakatipu and Wanaka are within the Mount Aspiring National Park.

Contributing to the beauty of New Zealand landscapes, especially in the South Island's mountains, is the clarity and brilliance of the light in a country whose atmosphere is still happily free of serious pollution. The drama that such light can impart to views in New Zealand is spectacularly apparent when a shaft of sunlight strikes the crest of the Remarkable Mountains near Queenstown *(right)* like a theatrical spotlight.

Many New Zealanders consider the beauty of Queenstown *(opposite, right)*, New Zealand's most popular tourist destination, to have been sullied by over-development. But many overseas visitors to Queenstown regard such opinions with disbelief. The development is restricted to one or two areas and the natural grandeur of the lake's vast basin is mostly unimpaired, certainly by overseas standards. The dramatic Remarkable Mountains loom above the waters of a lake which occupies a deep trough scooped by an ancient glacier between high mountains.

The jetboat was a New Zealand invention, and is now used to give visitors to Queenstown a thrilling ride on the Shotover River *(this page, top)* near Queenstown. Few riders, their hearts in their mouths as the boats scoot through impossibly narrow gaps or skim over treacherous shallows, have time to remember that in gold rush days last century, the Shotover yielded fabulous riches to miners willing to toil hard and endure great privations in the then wild region.

North of Lake Wakatipu, Lake Wanaka is less developed and draws fewer visitors, though it is of comparable splendour. At Glendhu Bay *(this page, above)* a popular campground occupies lake-front land among pines, behind the shore-line willows. Many New Zealanders have wonderful childhood memories of camping holidays at Glendhu Bay.

42

44

Fiordland National Park's 1.25 million hectares make it easily New Zealand's largest. Close to thirty per cent of New Zealand's land area is protected in national parks, forest parks and reserves, one of the highest percentages of any country in the world. One of the scenic highlights of Fiordland are the Sutherland Falls *(above)*, New Zealand's highest, which descend in three steps a total of 580 metres. They are seen here from the Milford Track. The boast that it is "the finest walk in the world" may be a little inflated, but not by much.

Fiordland is a maze of mountain ranges and deep river valleys and lakes, all sculpted by ice. Highest of the ranges are the Darrans *(opposite page, top)*. The fine view of them from the Key Summit is only a short walk above the Milford Road.

The forested valleys of Fiordland offer wonderful opportunities for short walks or longer tramps. This fine beech forest in the Eglinton Valley *(opposite page, lower left)* is only a short distance from the Milford Road.

The size of their packs indicates that these trampers in the Wilkin Valley *(opposite page, lower right)* in the Mount Aspiring National Park (which borders the Fiordland Park to the north) are on more than just a short stroll from their cars. Innumerable tracks, long and short, difficult and easy, make New Zealand a hiker's paradise.

Fiordland is a region of different moods: its water lies still in tranquil lakes, and also falls tempestuously in mountain rivers. Few who view the aptly named Falls Creek *(above)* leave without feeling better for the experience, soothed by the rhythm and sound of its cascades.

Though Lake Te Anau is large enough to be whipped up into storms, on a calm morning its waters lie absolutely still at the waterfront of the town of Te Anau *(left)*. Beyond, across the rugged, roadless mountains, the sea and the fiords which gave the region its name are surprisingly close.

Following pages: One of the most famous views in the world, not just New Zealand, is Fiordland's piece de resistance, Milford Sound. The impact of the view is not diminished by over-familiarity with pictures of it or by the number of visitors who crowd the pocket handkerchief of flat land at the head of the sound. Mitre Peak rises almost sheer to a height of 1,695 metres above the waters of the sound; below, sheer rock walls plunge 350 metres beneath the sea. Nowhere else in New Zealand has glacier ice fashioned so dramatic and beautiful a scene.

The orderly layout of central Dunedin *(above)* around its Octagon is clearly evident from the air. Like New Zealand's other coastal cities, Dunedin has an attractive setting—the head of Otago Harbour is visible upper left. But the beauty of Dunedin, more than that of any other New Zealand city (except perhaps Christchurch) derives also from its architecture. Dunedin was briefly, at the height of the Otago gold rush last century, the country's largest, wealthiest city. Early wealth and later quiet growth have left the city with a wonderful legacy of old buildings.

The Dunedin Railway Station *(opposite page, below),* built early this century, is New Zealand's finest railway station and in the opinion of some its finest building, full-stop. The building earned for its architect, George Troup, the nickname "Gingerbread George".

Terrace houses are a relatively unusual building form in New Zealand, where there is plenty of space for most families to have a detached house and section of their own. Dunedin's Stuart Street Terrace *(opposite page, above)* is as reminiscent of Victorian Scotland as parts of Christchurch are of Victorian England. The Terrace is a reminder that Dunedin had its mid nineteenth century origins as a Church of Scotland inspired settlement.

Though they live together in reasonable amity, Maori and Pakeha New Zealanders remain different people. The differences, which enrich New Zealand's social and cultural life, are apparent in the different explanations given for the Moeraki Boulders *(above)* on the Otago coast. To Pakeha they are concretions whose geological origin can be explained scientifically. To Maori they are the petrified gourds washed ashore when an ancestral canoe was wrecked on a nearby reef.

At the southern extremity of the South Island, the port town of Bluff is a windswept, even bleak place, the Bluff Hill affording only meagre protection from the gales that sweep in from the Southern Ocean. But from the air, wonderful patterns are evident in the estuary that deepens to Bluff Harbour *(right)*. The aluminium smelter on Tiwai Point, left centre, makes a valuable contribution to the New Zealand economy. Though at ground level the smelter hardly graces the view, from high up it is less intrusive on the scene.

On Stewart Island, human settlement is confined to a tiny corner around Half Moon Bay. The houses and cottages of the settlement straggle over a low ridge to the shores of Patterson Inlet. Seen from Observation Rock *(opposite page, bottom)*, the sheltered waters of the inlet stretch beyond the cottages and jetties of Golden Bay and Thule Beach into the wild uninhabited heart of Stewart Island.

A friendly rivalry exists across Cook Strait, the twenty-kilometre wide stretch of often turbulent water that separates the South Island from the North. The North Island has many more people — 2.5 million to the South's 880,000. But Southerners insist that what they lack by way of population, towns and cities, their island more than makes up for by the grandeur and greater beauty of its landscapes. To acknowledge there are differences between the islands is not to take sides in this rivalry. The North Island does have more cities and towns, large and small, and much of its farmland is more closely subdivided and densely populated. The South Island may have the country's highest mountain, (Aoraki/Mount Cook), but the North has its largest city (by far), Auckland. The South may have New Zealand's only significant glaciers, but the North has its only oil and gas fields. Though the North Island's beauty is less dramatic than the South's, it is appealing nonetheless. And of its mountains, lesser only when compared with the Southern Alps, Taranaki/Mount Egmont is indisputably one of the most beautiful volcanoes in the world. The predominant tones in many parts of the South are yellow, fawn and grey; many prefer the green tones of the North Island's peaceful rural landscape and forested ranges. And in many parts of the North Island, dairy cows on lush, verdant grass are more common than the sheep and beef cattle which graze the South Island's often sparser and yellower pastures.

One other significant difference between the South Island and the North is that in the North, the presence of New Zealand's indigenous people, the Maori, is more apparent than in the South. Although centuries ago, when the first Polynesians to reach New Zealand hunted the now extinct moa, a large flightless bird, there were probably more people in the South Island than the North, for most of New Zealand's history, there have been more Maori (and since European settlement, more people overall) in the North than in the South.

The far northern tip of the North Island, Cape Reinga *(opposite page),* is one of the most sacred places in Maori tradition as the place from which the spirits of the dead made their final departure for the underworld. Natural beauty has inspired New Zealand artists of many generations to create beauty of their own. The country's earliest artists, the Maori, took inspiration from the young fronds of the tree fern *(head of page),* a symbol of the unfolding of life, and motifs which are still seen in traditional and modern Maori art can be traced back to the curling frond.

On the east coast of Northland, the Bay of Islands is the cradle of modern New Zealand history, but many visit the Bay seeking not an understanding of the past so much as fun on the water. The Bay's intricate inlets, abundant beaches and island-studded waters afford unrivalled opportunities for boating, fishing and swimming. Piercy Rock *(opposite page, top left)* is one of the scenic highlights of a Bay of Islands cruise in boats like Tiger III. Just how popular the Bay of Islands is among "boaties" is evident in the number of yachts moored in Matauwhi Bay, near Russell, *(opposite page, bottom)*.

None of the North Island's myriad waterfalls can match the grandeur of falls found in the Southern Alps, but the Rainbow Falls, near Kerikeri, *(opposite page, top right)* have their own humbler beauty.

Over much of the North Island the dense mantle of forest that greeted the first human beings to reach these shores a thousand years ago has been stripped away, some by the Maori practising their slash-and-burn agriculture, most by the European settlers clearing land for pasture. Though many of the ravaged landscapes have healed since, great beauty was lost. Of the vast kauri forests of the northern parts of the North Island, only remnants now remain. But happily in these remnants, especially in the Waipoua Forest north of Dargaville, some magnificent kauri trees survive, including Tane Mahuta *(above),* the Lord of the Forest.

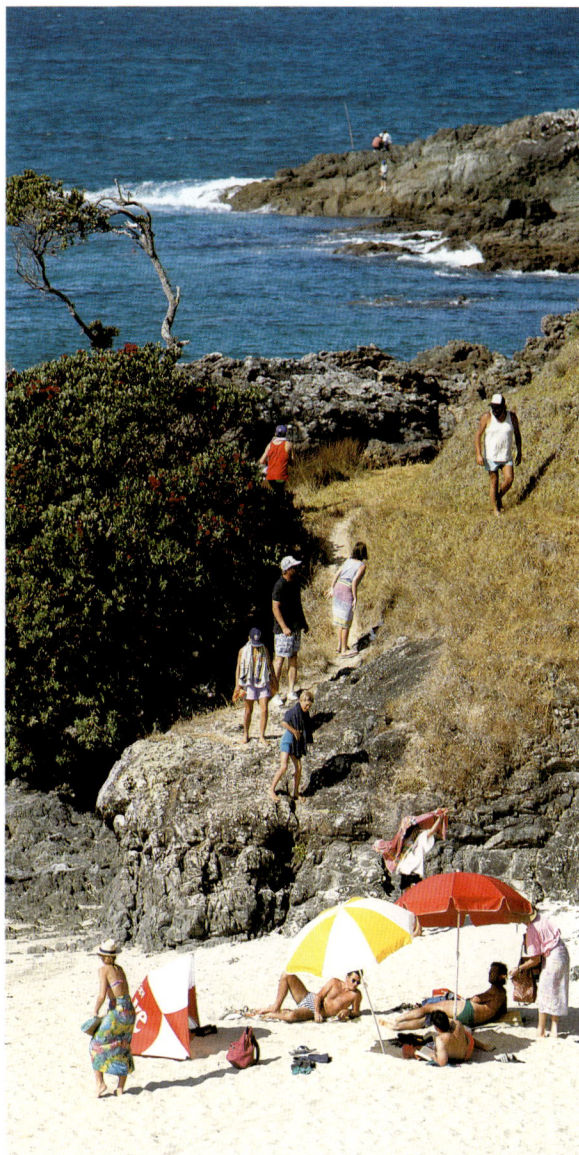

Contrasting dramatically with the sheltered bays and coves of the Bay of Islands is the broad, open sweep of Ninety Mile Beach *(above, left)* on the western side of the Far North's finger-like peninsula. The packed sand of the beach is hard enough for tour buses to speed visitors through the marvellous expanse of sea and sky.

Proof that New Zealand offers an extraordinary variety of landscapes within a small area is that the intimate sandy beach of Matai Bay *(above, right),* where bathers enjoy the protection of small rocky headlands and the shelter of the red-flowering pohutukawa, (known as the New Zealand Christmas tree because its flowering coincides with the festive season) is in the same part of the country as open and windswept Ninety Mile Beach.

The clouds massing over the land on the far side of the Kerikeri Inlet from Opito Bay *(left)* indicate that this is the part of New Zealand which looks north, to the tropical Pacific, while Bluff, some 1,500 kilometres further from the equator, looks south to the sub-antarctic.

In few places in New Zealand is the "sense of history" so palpable as at the Kerikeri Basin *(opposite page, below)*. Two of the oldest buildings in New Zealand, the Kemp House (1821–22) and the Stone Store (completed 1835–36), built by some of the earliest missionaries to come to New Zealand, stand on the shore of the Basin, above which is the site of a Maori pa. This was the scene of early and significant interaction between Maori and Pakeha, but where the missionaries' cutter once came up the river to the Basin, modern pleasure boats are now moored.

Inland from Kerikeri, near where the plough was first put to New Zealand soil, a warm climate and fertile soils have encouraged the planting of orchards *(opposite page, above)*, many of citrus trees which are protected against winds (from north to south New Zealand is a windy land) by shelter belts that make strong patterns when seen from the air.

The complexity of the Bay of Islands coastline and its attraction for those whose favourite summer pastimes are boating, fishing or swimming in these warm northern waters, is apparent in this aerial view of Otehei Bay and Urupuka-puka Island *(above)*. Near here, James Cook, on his first visit to New Zealand in 1769–70, anchored and gave the bay its name.

The little towns which grew up on the shores of the Bay of Islands in the 1820s and 1830s are now popular holiday destinations. Paihia *(above, left)* and Russell *(above, right)* face each other across a stretch of water and are linked by a ferry. But Paihia began its days as a sober, strait-laced missionary settlement, while Russell (then called Kororareka and known as "the hell-hole of the Pacific") was the roistering, rowdy haunt of whalers and traders, which the missionaries regarded with suspicion and distaste.

The Bay of Islands was the scene of the most significant event in New Zealand's history, the signing of the Treaty of Waitangi between the British Crown and chiefs of various Maori tribes on 6 February 1840. This compact was the foundation of New Zealand's modern bi-cultural society and its implications for New Zealand's national life are still being worked out. The treaty was signed in front of the Waitangi Treaty House *(left),* which still stands in its picturesque setting on a low headland looking out over the Bay of Islands.

Auckland is New Zealand's largest city, a bustling, vibrant, sprawling place whose inhabitants keep the wheels of the country's largest concentration of factories turning and who, people elsewhere in the country tend to think, are hedonistic pleasure-seekers who look with disdain on people who live in the southern provinces! Downtown Auckland *(above)* is a cluster of tall buildings on the southern shore of the Waitemata Harbour, spanned since 1959 by the Harbour Bridge, middle distance, used by commuters from the North Shore to reach their jobs in the city itself. Though Auckland is, architecturally, not a city of particular distinction or interest, its fine harbour, with bridge and marina *(opposite page, above)*, give it an attractive setting. Its familiar description "the city of sails" indicates that Aucklanders keen on sailing take full advantage of the harbour.

Even from populous Auckland, relatively wild and unfrequented places are easily accessible. Piha Beach, with its distinctive Lion Rock, *(opposite page, below)* is less than an hour's drive from the city's downtown heart and the haunt of surfers and holiday-makers. Some of these have "baches", as most New Zealanders call their holiday homes, nestled among the sandhills and scrub behind the beach.

Auckland is a city given over to cars, laced by motorways, but still has precincts and neighbourhoods attractive for pedestrians. Albert Park *(above right)* with its flower-beds, statuary and palms, is a favourite place for strolling. The site of a military barracks in Auckland's early days, the park is now overlooked by the tower of one of the older buildings of Auckland University.

Hamilton *(right, opposite page)*, somewhat unusually for New Zealand, is an inland city. The city straddles the Waikato River and is an industrial and business centre serving the farms of the fertile plains of the lower Waikato. (The river, at 425 kilometres, is New Zealand's longest.) The land was controversially confiscated from its Maori owners during the Land Wars of the 1860s and later developed as one of the country's premier dairying areas.

More typically, Tauranga and its satellite town, Mount Maunganui, are on the coast. Tauranga is an important port—from it are exported timber, pulp and paper derived from the huge exotic forests of the central North Island. But there is also a boat harbour at Tauranga *(above)* where small craft can shelter. "The Mount" (Mount Maunganui, in the background) guards one of the entrances to the Tauranga Harbour. Like the great majority of New Zealanders, those living in Tauranga and Mount Maunganui take advantage of their ready access to the sea. The surf at Mount Maunganui's Ocean Beach *(left)* draws swimmers from Tauranga and further afield.

East of Auckland, the thumb of the Coromandel Peninsula juts north, protecting the waters of the Hauraki Gulf, a paradise for boating. With a central spine of rugged ranges, the Coromandel has both sheltered bays and rocky headlands on each of its coasts. Te Ororoa Point *(above)* on the Coromandel's east coast, is exposed to the swells and storms of the open Pacific. But the Peninsula's east coast also has sheltered bays and harbours. The town of Whitianga *(opposite page, above)* has grown up on the shore of Mercury Bay, so named by James Cook when he called here in 1769 to observe a transit of Mercury. Ubiquitous pleasure boats find shelter in the river-mouth harbour.

Before Europeans came to New Zealand, the Coromandel Peninsula was densely forested and in the Coromandel ranges are some of the few remaining kauri forests. Even where the ancient forests are gone, as on the shores of Port Jackson *(opposite page, below),* the Coromandel is still a place of great beauty, with shore-loving pohutukawa below grassy hills.

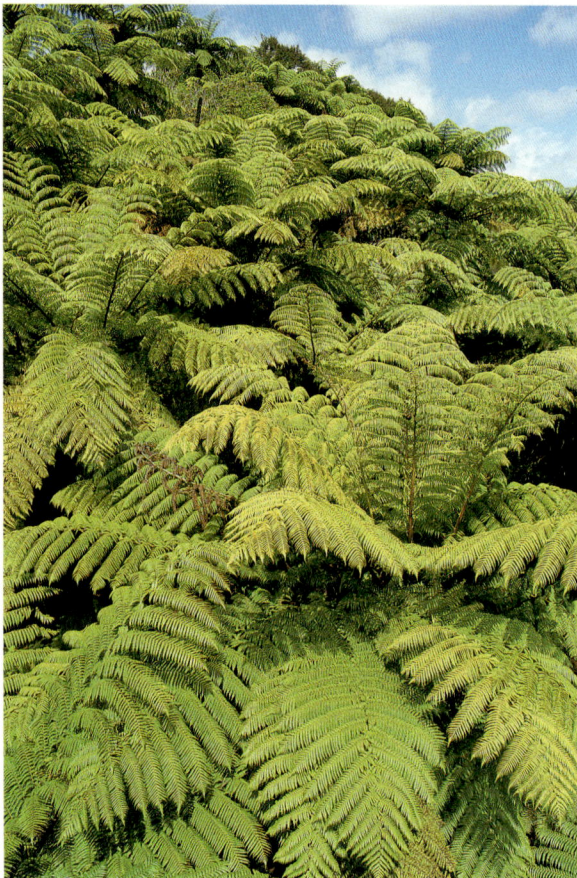

The many harbours of the Coromandel Peninsula, including the Whangapoua Harbour *(above)*, spread beautiful stretches of calm water against a background of rugged hills, on which the bush that escaped milling for timber or being burnt to create pasture still remains. The Coromandel lowlands were cleared and now support lush pasture on which dairy cows graze, outdoors year-round. The farmhouse on this Whangapoua Harbour dairy farm *(right)* is typically modest and in a typically New Zealand setting, with well-tended pasture in the foreground and forested ranges behind.

The artistry of nature is apparent in the massing of tree ferns *(left)* which grow in abundance on the hills of the Coromandel Peninsula and of Northland, where warmth and abundant rainfall encourage vegetation that has a hint of the tropical about it.

The peacefulness of many North Island landscapes is from one point of view deceptive, because much of the North Island is volcanic in origin. One of the most active of the country's volcanoes is White Island *(above)*, at the northern end of the broad volcanic zone which extends from the centre of the North Island out to sea off the Bay of Plenty coast. Its plume of smoke is often visible from the coast of the mainland. An attempt to mine sulphur on the island in the early twentieth century ended in disaster when an eruption overwhelmed the works, killing several workers.

But the violent origins of much of the North Island are scarcely apparent looking over the fertile green Waikato Plains *(left)*. The Waikato is an important horse-breeding area and the oval surrounded by pasture and crop land is a horse-training track.

On the Waikato's green pastures has been bred some of the fine horse-flesh which has given New Zealand an international reputation for its race horses, and which sustains a major domestic horse-racing industry. The Blandford Lodge Stud near Matamata *(right)* is a leading horse-breeding farm.

The country inland from the Bay of Plenty itself is gentle and kind (Cook gave the Bay its name when he was able to secure water, food and firewood with ease on his first visit to New Zealand). The coastline corresponding to this gentle country has sandy beaches and low headlands. Whanarua Bay *(left)* is one of the popular picnicking and camping spots along this coast. But to the east, where the broad curve of the Bay of Plenty turns north towards the rugged East Cape, with its high rough ranges inland from rocky shores, the coastline is more dramatic. Lottin Point *(above)* is on the eastern edge of the Bay of Plenty, not far from the East Cape itself.

The elegant sweep of beach of Hicks Bay *(right)* at the East Cape end of the Bay of Plenty, with an almost imperceptible swell coasting in from the South Pacific, epitomises the unrivalled opportunities New Zealanders still enjoy (even those living on the more populous North Island) to "escape from it all". So do the "baches" (holiday homes) on the empty Waihau Beach, on the East Coast, *(above, lower picture)*.

The Kaimai Ranges, still carrying forest on their steep flanks, separate the inland plains and hill country west of the Bay of Plenty from the coast. The wooden, iron-roofed house of this farm scene at Tapapa, near Rotorua, *(above, upper picture)* is the home of the family which owns and runs the farm. Single-family farms are still the norm in New Zealand where farmers and their families, although only fifteen percent of the population lives in the country, still consider themselves the backbone of the nation.

The view south across Lake Taupo *(opposite page, below right)* takes in the volcanic mountains at the centre of the North Island, including the loftiest, Mount Ruapehu, left, and more shapely Mount Ngauruhoe, right. Lake Taupo itself occupies a vast volcanic caldera. Eruptions from the caldera in the distant past have coated much of the North Island with volcanic ash or pumice.

At the highest point of the North Island is the crater lake of Mount Ruapehu *(above),* southernmost of the volcanoes of the central North Island. Ruapehu is still intermittently active and the waters of the Crater Lake, though surrounded by ice and snow, are usually warm. In 1953, ice damming the lake gave way and the lahar which roared down the Whangaehu River swept away a railway bridge at Tangiwai and caused one of New Zealand's worst disasters.

Also still active, intermittently but more vigorously than Ruapehu, Mount Ngauruhoe *(opposite page, below left)* is younger and more symmetrical than its larger neighbour.

The marina at Taupo *(opposite page, above)* is close to where the Waikato River leaves the lake to begin its long journey to the sea. With pleasure boats riding peacefully at their moorings on a calm evening, it is hard to credit that the basin occupied by the lake, New Zealand's largest, had such violent origins.

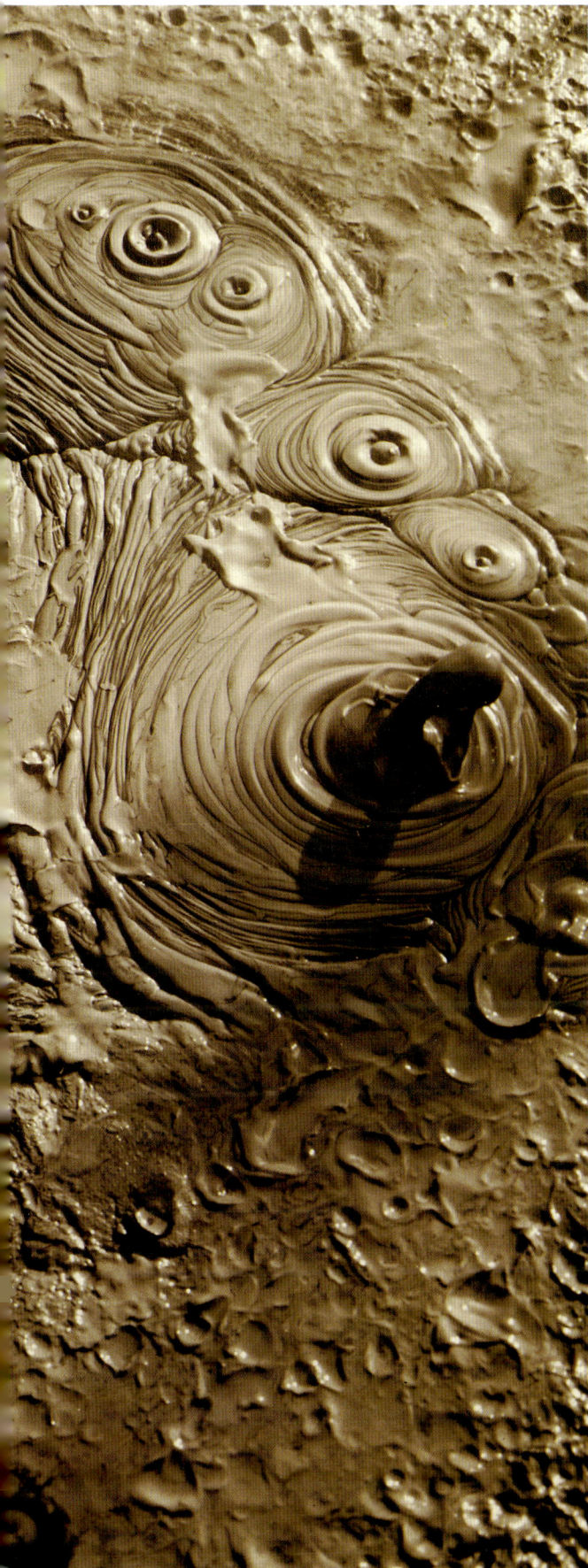

North of the central mountains and Lake Taupo, the volcanic zone takes on a different character. The Rotorua thermal zone is characterised by geysers, mud pools and hot springs and lakes. Largest of the geysers is Pohutu *(above)* in the Whakarewarewa thermal field, close to the city of Rotorua. Rotorua has long been a tourist destination and though few visitors now come expecting cures from its thermal waters, it still attracts those eager to view its spectacular natural features, including the patterns of its boiling mud pools *(left)*.

The summit of Mount Tarawera *(left, this page)* can be visited on foot or by four-wheel-drive. The chasm is a chilling reminder of the awesome power of the volcanic zone. The 1886 eruption which rent the mountain destroyed three Maori villages, killed more than 150 people, and obliterated the famous pink and white terraces.

The silica deposits of Warbrick Terrace *(opposite page, above)* in the Waimangu thermal valley are a pale shadow of the pink and white terraces which were destroyed in the 1886 Tarawera eruption, but fascinating in their own right. The Waimangu Valley is an extension of the line of vulcanism that runs across Tarawera's summit.

The rivers and lakes of the central North Island from the southern side of Lake Taupo to north of Rotorua are a world-famous trout fishery. The trout at Rainbow Springs *(opposite page, below)* are not for catching but for viewing by visitors.

New Zealand's great forest trees provided a valuable raw material for Maori artists and artisans. Wood carvings, of great intricacy and power, are generally regarded as the highest achievements of Maori art. The meeting house, carved and decorated inside with woven tukutuku panels and painted kowhaiwhai patterns, is one of the most magnificent expressions of the Maori imagination and the focal point of the social and spiritual life of tribal groups. The meeting house Tokanganui-a-noho at Te Kuiti *(above, left)* is more than a hundred years old.

Rotorua is the centre of the powerful and numerous Arawa confederation of Maori tribes. It has long been where most visitors to New Zealand get a taste of the fascinating traditional culture of New Zealand's "tangata whenua", the people of the land, the first to reach New Zealand's distant shores. Though most Maori now live urban lives similar to those of their Pakeha compatriots, theirs is still a strong and proud culture. The graceful poi dance being performed in a meeting house at Whakarewarewa *(right)* is the women's equivalent of the fearsome haka of the men *(above, right),* performed in olden times before battle to intimidate opponents and inspire bravery and valour in hand-to-hand combat.

Thermal activity and Maori culture are the main draw-cards of the Rotorua region, but it is also an area of great scenic beauty, of bush-fringed streams *(left)* and peaceful lakes, among them Lake Okataina *(above)*, not far from Rotorua itself, enfolded in forest-clad hills.

Much of the hill country of the central North Island was cleared of its natural forest late last century and early this to create pasture. Today these steep, grassed hills are grazed mostly by large flocks of sheep. Near Raetihi *(above)* a farmer has yarded his flock near the woolshed,where the sheep are shorn each year. The woolshed is now as indigenous to and as typical of New Zealand as the carved meeting house of the Maori.

The North Island hill country, whether still clothed in native bush or cleared and in pasture, lacks the grandeur of other parts of New Zealand, but in the peaceful folds of secluded valleys are attractive waterfalls. The Papakorito Falls *(right)* are in the Urewera National Park, where forests on some of the rougher country which escaped the settlers' axes and fires are protected from any future harm.

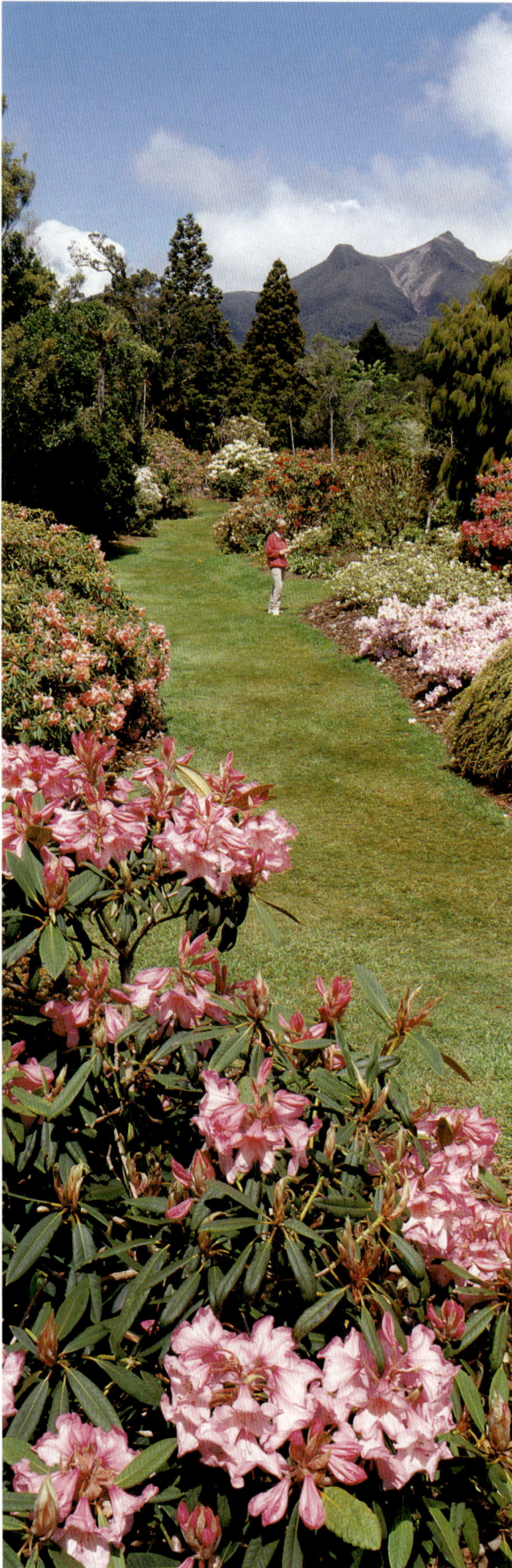

Solitary, a cone of nearly perfect symmetry, Taranaki/ Mount Egmont rises above its gradually sloping ring plain *(right, above)*. The plain was once covered with dense bush, but now the ample rainfall falling on the rich volcanic soil sustains the pastures that make the province of Taranaki a leading dairying region. The ranges and lower slopes of the mountain itself are still bush-covered and protected as national park.

Not far from New Plymouth, on the lower slopes of a foothill range of Taranaki/Mount Egmont, rhododendrons flourish in a bush setting at Pukeiti *(left)*. After 150 years of European settlement of New Zealand, some of its most pleasing scenery blends native and introduced, as the rhododendrons here show to advantage against the sombre but varied greens of the bush.

The story of much of the inland North Island is one of wresting pasture from bush. Clearing of bush from hill country continued well into the twentieth century. On hill country inland from Tokomaru Bay on the East Coast of the North Island *(right, below)* the country still looks raw and newly won from the forest.

The "provincial" cities of the North Island sometimes seem sleepy, conservative places. But appearances can be deceiving, and many of the country's secondary cities (no more than large towns by most international standards) have surprisingly sophisticated and active social and cultural lives. The Esplanade Gardens of Palmerston North, chief city of the Manawatu region, *(above)* have a settled, well-tended air. New Zealanders are inveterate gardeners, and their love of gardening is evident in the public gardens of cities and towns, as well as in private gardens around their houses.

Gisborne, rather isolated from the rest of the country, has the distinction of being where James Cook first landed in New Zealand and where the first significant contact between Maori and Pakeha occurred. This was not far from Gisborne's boat harbour *(left)*. The town is a river port, serving the North Island's East Coast region.

On the east coast of the North Island, south of Gisborne, Napier is the capital of the province of Hawkes Bay, though its vigorous neighbour Hastings is as large and as economically important as Napier. The town centre of Napier viewed from Bluff Hill *(above)* was levelled by a devastating earthquake in 1932. Rebuilt during the Depression, Napier is fast gaining a worldwide reputation for its wonderful collection of Art Deco buildings.

Some of the country's oldest vineyards are in Hawkes Bay and though grape-growing has spread to other parts of the country, Hawkes Bay still has a flourishing wine-making industry. New Zealand's domestic architecture has developed its own distinctive style, which is apparent in this dramatic house set in a Hawkes Bay vineyard *(right)*.

Much of New Zealand's coastline is wild and treacherous. It is well-supplied with lighthouses to warn mariners of danger and guide them safely to port. Many of these lighthouses are inaccessible, but one of the finest, at Castlepoint on the Wairarapa coast *(above, left)*, which dates from 1913, can be reached by road and has a holiday settlement nearby. The dramatic headland was named by Captain Cook when he sailed past it in 1770 because it looked to him, from the sea, like a castle.

Fewer overseas visitors visit the Wanganui River *(above, right)* now than at the turn of the century when it was touted as "the Rhine of New Zealand". It was not really an apt comparison, for the Wanganui is appealing not for its castles or riverside villages but for the magnificence of its wild scenery as it snakes through complicated, bush-clad ranges. Canoes and other pleasure boats open this superbly scenic area, much of it inaccessible by road, to adventuresome visitors.

New Zealand's capital since 1865 (when the seat of government was shifted from Auckland to a more central location), Wellington has a superb setting on a sheltered harbour that opens onto Cook Strait. New Zealand's government is housed in a rather odd collection of buildings *(left)*, the Victorian Gothic General Assembly Library to the right, the half-completed Edwardian Baroque Parliament Building in the centre, and the modern Executive Wing, popularly known as the Beehive, to the left.

Most of Wellington is built over steep hills surrounding its fine harbour. To reach the suburb of Kelburn from downtown, commuters and shoppers use the quaint cable car *(above)* which has run up and down its steep track since 1902. Beyond the tall buildings of the central city are houses perched on steep hillsides and beyond them again the Orongorongo Ranges on the far side of the harbour. It is typical of New Zealand that wild, rugged ranges form the background to a major city, that urban dwellers can look up from busy streets to see what the country was like before people ever arrived. The unique life styles of New Zealand are founded on this rare and valued feature of the country— that wild beauty is readily accessible from sophisticated late twentieth century cities.

Designed by Warren Jacobs and John Burt
Finished Artwork by John Burt Graphics
Christchurch
Film positives made in Hong Kong
Printed and bound in Hong Kong

Published by Kowhai Publishing Ltd.
RD 1 Lyttelton and 10 Peacock Street,
Auckland

First published in 1995

ISBN 0–908598–62–9